ONE: THE EMPEROR'S NEW CLOTHES

We bet on our lives and we bet on the horses
In that upstairs apartment
On Orlando and 4th
And the rent was due and the rent man was knocking
Like a Chinese proverb
We were always searching

Nightlife's a no win but nobody noticed
How we killed off the bottles
Looking good on the surface
The dog days barked and the house cat got old
We were Bonnie and Clyde
In the emperor's new clothes

And the tears never came
They just stayed in our eyes
We refused to admit that we wore this disguise
Every inch of us growing
Like Pinocchio's nose
As we walked around in the emperor's new clothes

We flew by our wits and by the seat of our pants
In the state of illusion
In the nation of chance
And the repo was hauling the wreck we'd been driving
As the dashboard Madonna
Smiled back at us kindly

We cheated the system never batting an eyelid
Seeing only the good
Through the holes in our shoes
And our halos were rusty but we wore them proudly
We were two little gods
In the emperor's new clothes

And the tears never came
They just stayed in our eyes
We refused to admit that we wore this disguise
Every inch of us growing
Like Pinocchio's nose
As we walked around in the emperor's new clothes

solo

We were Bonnie and Clyde
In the emperor's new clothes

And the tears never came
They just stayed in our eyes
We refused to admit that we wore this disguise
Every inch of us growing
Like Pinocchio's nose
As we walked around in the emperor's new clothes
Emperor's new clothes
Emperor's new clothes

TWO: DARK DIAMOND

Oh, I'm a dark diamond
I've turned hard and cold
Once was a jewel with fire in my soul
There's two sides of a mirror
One I couldn't break through
Stayed trapped on the inside, wound up losing you

Tell me how does it work?
How do you make things fit
Spent all my life trying to get it right
I've put it together and it falls apart
I thought to myself I might understand
But when the wall's built
And the heart hardens
You get a dark diamond
Dark diamond

Oh, I'm a dark diamond
But you're something else
You read me more than I read myself
The one star I could count on
Only comet I could trust
You burnt through my life to the true meaning of love

Tell me how does it work?
How do you make things fit
Spent all my life trying to get it right
I've put it together and it falls apart
I thought to myself I might understand
But when the wall's built
And the heart hardens
You get a dark diamond
Dark diamond

solo

Tell me how does it work?
How do you make things fit
Spent all my life trying to get it right
I've put it together and it falls apart
I thought to myself I might understand
But when the wall's built
And the heart hardens
You get a dark diamond
Dark diamond

Dark diamond
You get a dark diamond
Dark diamond
Dark diamond
You get a dark diamond
Dark diamond
You get a dark diamond
Dark diamond

THREE: LOOK MA, NO HANDS

I'll take a rainy day
To make a champagne shower
Poach some horn and tusk
To build an ivory tower

Been to Philadelphia
The day it was closed
I walked to New Orleans
Down a Louisiana road

The skeletons they hung from the bushes and the trees
But not a skull among 'em said boo to me
In a time of wine and cheap cigars
I'm on top of the world
Top of the world Ma

Look Ma no hands
Look Ma ain't life grand
I'm a super power; I'm a handy man
Didn't I turn out, didn't I turn out to be
Everything you wanted Ma
Ain't you proud of me

It takes a silver tongue
To have the Midas touch
Not your alchemist
Making gold from rust

Been down in Roswell
When the Martians came
I sailed to Mandeville
Across Lake Pontchartrain

Look Ma no hands
Look Ma ain't life grand
I'm a super power; I'm a handy man
Didn't I turn out, didn't I turn out to be
Everything you wanted Ma
Ain't you proud of me

solo

The skeletons they hung from the bushes and trees
But not a skull among 'em said boo to me
In a time of wine and cheap cigars
I'm on top of the world
I'm on top of the world Ma

Look Ma no hands
Look Ma ain't life grand
I'm a super power; I'm a handy man
Didn't I turn out, didn't I turn out to be
Everything you wanted Ma
Ain't you proud of me

Didn't I turn out, didn't I turn out to be
Everything you wanted Ma
Ain't you proud of me

FOUR: AMERICAN TRIANGLE

Seen him playing in his backyard
Young boy just starting out
So much history in this landscape
So much confusion, so much doubt

Been there drinking on that front porch
Angry kids mean and dumb
Looks like a painting that blue skyline
God hates fags where we come from

Western skies don't make it right
Home of the brave don't make no sense
I've seen a scarecrow wrapped in wire
Left to die on a high ridge fence
It's a cold, cold wind, it's a cold, cold wind
It's a cold wind blowing, Wyoming

See two coyotes running down a deer
Hate what we don't understand
You pioneers give us your children
But it's your blood that stains their hands

Western skies don't make it right
Home of the brave don't make no sense
I seen a scarecrow wrapped in wire
Left to die on a high ridge fence
It's a cold, cold wind, it's a cold, cold wind
It's a cold wind blowing, Wyoming

Somewhere that road forks up ahead
To Ignorance and innocence
Three lives drift on different winds
Two lives ruined one life spent
Western skies don't make it right
Home of the brave don't make no sense
I've seen a scarecrow wrapped in wire
Left to die on a high ridge fence
It's a cold, cold wind, it's a cold, cold wind
It's a cold wind blowing, Wyoming

It's a cold, cold wind, it's a cold, cold wind
It's a cold wind blowing, blowing
Wyoming

FIVE: ORIGINAL SIN

Oh, it's carnival night
And they're stringing the lights around you
Hanging paper angels
Painting little devils on the roof

Oh the furnace wind
Is a flickering of wings about your face
In a cloud of incense
Yea, it smells like Heaven in this place

I can't eat, can't sleep
Still I hunger for you when you look at me

That face, those eyes
All the sinful pleasures deep inside

Tell me how, you know now, the ways and means of getting in
Underneath my skin,
Oh you were always my original sin
And tell me why, I shudder inside, every time we begin
This dangerous game
Oh you were always my original sin

A dream will fly
The moment that you open up your eyes
A dream is just a riddle
Ghosts from every corner of your life

Up in the balcony
All the Romeo's are bleeding for your hand
Blowing theater kisses
Reciting lines they don't understand

I can't eat, can't sleep
Still I hunger for you when you look at me
That face, those eyes
All the sinful pleasures deep inside
Tell me how, you know now, the ways and means of getting in
Underneath my skin,
Oh you were always my original sin
And tell me why, I shudder inside, every time we begin
This dangerous game
Oh you were always my original sin
Tell me how, you know now, the ways and means of getting in
Underneath my skin,
Oh you were always my original sin
And tell me why, I shudder inside, every time we begin
This dangerous game
Oh you were always my original sin

SIX: BIRDS

There's some things I don't have now
Some things I don't talk about
These things are between myself and I
In my thick skull the joker hides

There's consequences I'm scared to taste
Cold hard truths I can't face
These days are different than the past
Reflections change in the looking glass

And everywhere I look there's something to learn
A sliver of truth from every bridge we burn
A hatful of quarters and a naked song
Don't answer the question of where we belong

How come birds
Don't fall from the sky when they die?
How come birds
Always look for a quiet place to hide
These words
Can't explain what I feel inside?

Like birds I need a quiet place to hide

These independent moves I make
This confidence I try to fake
You can hear the beating of my heart
But not a feather falling in the dark

And everything I hear never makes any sense
Another old prophet perched on the fence
A cupful of pencils and a self help guru
Don't answer the question of what I am to you

How come birds
Don't fall from the sky when they die?
How come birds
Always look for a quiet place to hide
These words
Can't explain what I feel inside?
Like birds I need a quiet place to hide

solo

How come birds
Don't fall from the sky when they die?
How come birds
Always look for a quiet place to hide
These words
Can't explain what I feel inside?
Like birds I need a quiet place to hide

SEVEN: I WANT LOVE

I want love but it's impossible
A man like me's so irresponsible
A man like me is dead in places
Other men feel liberated

And I can't love shot full of holes
Don't feel nothing I just feel cold
Don't feel nothing just old scars
Toughening up around my heart

But I want love
Just a different kind
I want love
Won't break me down
Won't brick me up
Won't fence me in
I want a love
That don't mean a thing
That's the love I want
I want love

I want love on my own terms
After everything I've ever learned
Me I carry too much baggage
Oh, man I've seen so much traffic

But I want love
Just a different kind

I want love
Won't break me down
Won't brick me up
Won't fence me in
I want a love
That don't mean a thing
That's the love I want
I want love
So bring it on I've been bruised
Don't give me love that's clean and smooth
I'm ready for the rougher stuff
No sweet romance, I've had enough

solo

A man like me's dead in places
Other men feel liberated

But I want love
Just a different kind
I want love
Won't break me down
Won't brick me up
Won't fence me in
I want a love
That don't mean a thing
That's the love I want
I want love

I want love
Just a different kind
I want love
Won't break me down
Won't brick me up
Won't fence me in
I want a love
That don't mean a thing
That's the love I want
I want love

EIGHT: THE WASTELAND

Some days I think it's all a dream
The things I've done, the places that I've been
This life of mine seemed surreal at times
Wasted days and nights in someone else's mind

Could it be I'm not for real?
I've slapped my face to check out how I feel
There's hostages to prove it's true
Who lives behind the mask was never proved

Come on Robert Johnson
Though we're worlds apart
You and I know what it's like
With the devil in our heart
You sold your soul at the crossroads
Kept a little of mine on hand
I'm wading out this muddy water
Been stranded in the Wasteland

Rattling chains all around my bed
Ghosts can laugh but they're already dead
I'm not dying and I'm far from gone
The blues man spent his candle but his pain lives on

Come on Robert Johnson
Though we're worlds apart
You and I know what it's like
With the devil in our heart
You sold your soul at the crossroads
Kept a little of mine on hand
I'm wading out this muddy water
Been stranded in the Wasteland

solo

Come on Robert Johnson
Though we're worlds apart
You and I know what it's like
With the devil in our heart
You sold your soul at the crossroads
Kept a little of mine on hand
I'm wading out this muddy water
Been stranded in the Wasteland

Come on Robert Johnson
Though we're worlds apart
You and I know what it's like
With the devil in our heart
You sold your soul at the crossroads
Kept a little of mine on hand
I'm wading out this muddy water
Been stranded in the Wasteland

In the Wasteland

NINE: BALLAD OF THE BOY IN THE RED SHOES

I'm stoned in the twilight
Screaming on the inside
Give me your water
Help me survive

Gonna miss the sunlight
When I lose my eyesight
Give me my red shoes
I want to dance
They searched for an answer
But that old man wouldn't listen
Back then I was handsome
Back then he was ignorant

And shave off the years now
It's all inside my head
The boy in the red shoes is dancing by my bed
Put them in a box somewhere
Put them in a drawer
Take my red shoes
I can't wear them anymore

Had garlands in the wings back then

All the pretty little things back then
Calling out my name
Oh what fame brings

After curtain calls and bows
I can't see the front row now
Hand me my red shoes
Just one more time

They pushed aside our presence
They refused to go the distance
Back then I was Sigmund
Back then he wouldn't listen

And shave off the years now
It's all inside my head
The boy in the red shoes is dancing by my bed
Put them in a box somewhere
Put them in a drawer
Take my red shoes
I can't wear them anymore

solo

They pushed aside our presence
They refused to go the distance
Back then I was Sigmund
Back then he wouldn't listen
Back then I was handsome
Back then he was ignorant

And shave off the years now
It's all inside my head
The boy in the red shoes is dancing by my bed
Put them in a box somewhere
Put them in a drawer
Take my red shoes
I can't wear them anymore

Put them in a box somewhere
Put them in a drawer
Take my red shoes
I can't wear them anymore

Take my red shoes
I can't wear them anymore
Take my red shoes
I can't wear them anymore

TEN: LOVE HER LIKE ME

You can take her
Make her change her name
You and your old money
Dance around the flame
But you can never, never love her like me

You can charm her
Calm her when she's wild
Show a little comfort
Play with her inner child
But you can never, never love her like me

So I just close my eyes and steal her away when you sleep
Sneak her in my dreams every single day of the week
You may have her in real world but if you could only see
How we rock this room in the twilight zone
And you can never, never love her like me

You can warm her
Charm her with your style
I know you convinced her
She's the love of your life
And no, you'll never, never love her like me

You can bless her
Keep her conscience clean
You can undress her
Go all the places I've been
But you'll never, never love her like me

So I just close my eyes and steal her away when you sleep
Sneak her in my dreams every single day of the week
You may have her in real world but if you could only see
How we rock this room in the twilight zone
And you can never, never love her like me

So I just close my eyes and steal her away when you sleep
Sneak her in my dreams every single day of the week
You may have her in the real world but if you could only see
How we rock this room in the twilight zone
And you can never, never, never, never, never
Love her like me

Love her like me

Love her like me

ELEVEN: MANSFIELD

It's a case I guess of paradise lost
Ten years back on the hands of the clock
In that little house on Mansfield
On your old block
Sometimes the magic of the past is all we've got

Just you and me at a crossroads then
Ain't it funny how we were old friends
Accidentally thrown together
Did we intend
To be the romantic novel you never want to end

And it's the contact of the eye that meets across a crowded room
And how I kind of wound up the lyrics to your tune
You said, "Funny but it feels like I've known you all my life
And how it might feel to kiss you on the mouth tonight"

In between the Star of David and the California moon
The Santa Ana winds blew warm into your room
We were crazy, wild and running
Blind to the change to come
In that little house on Mansfield
We'd wake at the break of dawn
In an Indian summer gone

In the candlelight I can recall
Your naked shadow looking ten feet tall
Like a wild pony dancing
Along the wall
Off balance I found love the only place to fall

And it's the contact of the eye that meets across a crowded room
And how I kind of wound up the lyrics to your tune
You said, "Funny but it feels like I've known you all my life
And how it might feel to kiss you on the mouth tonight"

In between the Star of David and the California moon
The Santa Ana winds blew warm into your room
We were crazy, wild and running
Blind to the change to come
In that little house on Mansfield
We'd wake at the break of dawn
In an Indian summer gone

Wake at the break of dawn
In an Indian summer gone
Wake at the break of dawn
In an Indian summer gone
At the break of dawn

At the break of dawn

At the break of dawn

At the break of dawn

TWELVE: THIS TRAIN DON'T STOP THERE ANYMORE

You may not believe it
But I don't believe in miracles anymore
And when I think about it
I don't believe I ever did for sure
All the things I've said in songs
All the purple prose you bought from me
Realities just black and white
The sentimental things I'd write
Never meant that much to me

I used to be the main express
All steam and whistles heading west
Picking up my pain from door to door
Riding on the Storyline
Furnace burning overtime
But this train don't stop
This train don't stop
This train don't stop there anymore

You don't need to hear it
But I'm dried up and sick to death of love
If you need to know it
I never really understood that stuff
All the stars and bleeding hearts
All the tears that welled up in my eyes
Never meant a thing to me
Read 'em as they say and weep
I've never felt enough to cry

I used to be the main express
All steam and whistles heading west
Picking up my pain from door to door
Riding on the Storyline
Furnace burning overtime
But this train don't stop
This train don't stop
This train don't stop there anymore

When I say that I don't care
It really means my engines breaking down
The chisel chips my heart again
The granite cracks beneath my skin
I crumble into pieces on the ground

I used to be the main express
All steam and whistles heading west
Picking up my pain from door to door
Riding on the Storyline
Furnace burning overtime
But this train don't stop
This train don't stop
This train don't stop there anymore

But this train don't stop
This train don't stop
This train don't stop there anymore

ELTON JOHN
SONGS FROM THE WEST COAST
piano vocal guitar

Published 2001
© International Music Publications Ltd
Griffin House 161 Hammersmith Road London W6 8BS England

Production Anna Joyce
Folio Design Dominic Brookman
Music Arranged by Artemis Music Ltd
Photography by Sam Taylor-Wood
Special thanks to Mercury Music

THE EMPEROR'S NEW CLOTHES

Words by Bernie Taupin
Music by Elton John

DARK DIAMOND

Words by Bernie Taupin
Music by Elton John

LOOK MA, NO HANDS

Words by Bernie Taupin
Music by Elton John

15

AMERICAN TRIANGLE

Words by Bernie Taupin
Music by Elton John

1. Seen him play-ing in his back - yard:
a young boy just start-ing out.

BIRDS

Words by Bernie Taupin
Music by Elton John

some things I don't have now, some things I don't talk a-bout, these

ORIGINAL SIN

Words by Bernie Taupin
Music by Elton John

2. A dream will fly_____ _____ Tell me how,-

I WANT LOVE

Words by Bernie Taupin
Music by Elton John

I want love____ but it's im - pos - si - ble:____

Verse 3:
(Instrumental)
A man like me is dead in places
Other men feel liberated.

And I want love *etc.*

THE WASTELAND

Words by Bernie Taupin
Music by Elton John

BALLAD OF THE BOY IN THE RED SHOES

Words by Bernie Taupin
Music by Elton John

Put them in a box some - where, put them in a drawer.

Take my red shoes, I can't wear them a - ny - more.

2. Had

LOVE HER LIKE ME

Words by Bernie Taupin
Music by Elton John

take her, make her change her name.___ You___ and your old mon-ey dance a-
(2.) warm her, charm her with your style.___ I know you con-vinced her she's the

MANSFIELD

Words by Bernie Taupin
Music by Elton John

Wake_____ at the break_ of dawn____ in an

Ind - ian sum - - - mer gone.____

(2° etc., ad lib. vocal)

Repeat to fade

THIS TRAIN DON'T STOP THERE ANYMORE

Words by Bernie Taupin
Music by Elton John

1. You may not be-lieve it, but I don't be-lieve in mi-ra-cles a-ny-more.
(2.) don't need to hear it, but I'm dried up and sick to death of love.